MW00789924

A RIVERFRONT TOWN By

The WACCAMAW RIVER

ISBN 0-9767079-2-6

Reflections of Life, Then and Now.

As seen from my perspective, and from my vantage point.

ISBN 0-9767079-2-6

Contents

Introduction

There is a lovely old historic Riverfront Town by the Waccamaw River. Conway, S.C. is that lovely old historic Riverfront Town that was founded in 1734 and settled around 1735 as Kingston Township, and it later became Conway borough. The Horry County museum has records and artifacts showing that the area was actually inhabited by Indians over 12,000 years ago. Conway is now the county seat of Horry County.

Conway is located along the Waccamaw River and is about 14 miles slightly northwest of Myrtle Beach. The Myrtle Beach Grand Strand area is now a major tourist attraction with many tourists from all over the country and world coming each year. The tourists and visitors enjoy the many attractions and the wonderful beaches all up and down the Myrtle Beach Grand Strand. Myrtle Beach was once called New Town and was a summer retreat for Conway residents. Now the whole world knows about the wonderful beaches along the Atlantic Ocean all up and down the Grand Strand. And the locals also know of other isolated retreats nearby.

The old county courthouse is located in Conway, although now there is a new courthouse right behind it. The old courthouse is a historic building that has been restored; and there are many other historic houses, buildings and places in Conway and some are on the National Historic Register and are being preserved. A few of these historic places are documented herein, but there are many more that one can see upon a visit to the town. The marina is right by the river and there are river tours on a riverboat, or you can rent a boat, etc.

I was born and raised in Conway, and it was a small farm town back in the fifties. There were many small family farms and we worked in the summers harvesting tobacco and cotton to obtain some money before school started. That way of life is all but gone now, and the town is growing and growing with new developments all over the place. It is now difficult to determine where Myrtle Beach ends and Conway begins if you're driving on highway 501 between Myrtle Beach and Conway.

Horry County has a year round population of about 200,000 and Conway has a population of about 15,000. In the summer time with all the tourists and visitors are on the Myrtle Beach Grand Strand the population swells to well over a half million and constantly growing. There is so much new construction in the area as many people from all over are coming here to buy second homes.

That lovely old historic Riverfront Town called Conway has been one of the best kept secrets near the Myrtle Beach Grand Strand area. It is so close to everything, yet offers a seclusion with peace and tranquility that so many of us like to enjoy, especially we retired folks. We can leave our little peaceful abodes and head toward the Atlantic Ocean and be tourists, or we can remain in our little quaint town and enjoy a country outing in the parks or outing on the river, marina or many other shops, restaurants and various attractions.

The Waccamaw River

The Waccamaw River is a mighty and ferocious black water river that runs by Conway. The Main street bridge crosses the Waccamaw River, and it is a serene and beautiful sight as you approach Conway coming on highway 501 businesses. You can see and feel the mighty Waccamaw River roaring beneath you as you cross the bridge coming into town. As you get across the bridge you will see a different view for a downtown area, as you will be able to see oak trees in the distance. The bridge has been beautifully restored and as you come off the bridge at the first stop light will be City Hall with the big town clock proudly standing out front keeping time.

I have seen this scene many times and each time it seems more serene. I've always loved the Waccamaw River since I was a young kid, and the Waccamaw River is one of the few black water rivers in America and in the world. The marina and boardwalk is downtown near the river and we've enjoyed the river for many years, and have seen many generations on the river for decades.

The Waccamaw River runs all the way down to Georgetown County and passes Sandy Island on the east side. The residents of Sandy Island must go across the Waccamaw River to get to their homes on the island. I spent many summers on Sandy Island as I was growing up as my father was born and raised on the island. I have known about and enjoyed the wonderful black waters of the Waccamaw River for over half a century, and it still amazes me with its wonders. The river runs past many towns along the way including Conway.

3

That Lovely Old Historic Riverfront Town

For centuries many generations have called this riverfront town home. Many go away but seem to always return to their serene old riverfront town by the Waccamaw River. It has been said that when one grows up in the county there is something about the dirt that they walk on that calls them back home to the county even after they're moved away for decades. There is something unique about growing up in a small town with a small town image, and it's something that lingers with one in a good way for a lifetime.

I can certainly attest to the fact that I was glad to get back to my hometown of Conway after being away working for over four decades in California. Although it was nice and pleasant where I was, I felt a compelling need to return to my roots to continue to record some of the wonderful experiences I had so many decades ago growing up in such a historic old town.

I have watched the area and town grow and change over the decades that I was away. There is now a tremendous growth in the area and in town that I knew was coming someday. This treasure of a little town is still a great place to grow up in and even better to retire in. I realized at a very young age that this little old town was overflowing with many wonderful places and scenes. There are just some things that an artist sees when others just seem to pass them by. I always noticed the old oak trees as I was growing up. I also noticed the unique and one of a kind old houses, churches, cemeteries, moss tree laden streets, lakes and rivers. I had taken a correspondence art course while I was in high school so many decades ago.

The population back in those days was less than 5,000 and everyone knew everyone in their neighborhoods, so to speak or at least knew of most everyone. Communities were smaller and closer knit then, but the hospitality is still there even today in what is a larger population. We only had one small radio station in town that we could get, and it was WLAT a 5,000 watt station, and that station is still on the air today along with many other stations in the county.

The Greyhound and Trailways bus systems were the main sources of mass transportation in the fifties when I was growing up there. Downtown was the only major shopping area for miles around, as this was before the days of shopping centers, and where in town was where most people resided. You could see and meet almost everyone shopping downtown on a Saturday afternoon, and shopping at the dime store was one of the things I enjoyed when I went shopping with my mother on a nice spring or summer afternoon. The memories are so vivid that it seems like just yesterday that it all happened.

The spring and early summer was an especially nice time, and the air was like a natural forest breeze. I often rode my bicycle from our house halfway across town to work. I always kept two bicycles and one of them had a basket on it for when I rode downtown to pick up some groceries for my parents. I was a pretty good bicycle rider and it didn't take me long to ride the couple of miles to get downtown. I also worked on and did all the maintenance on my bicycles as there wasn't much to a bicycle in the fifties. I also did my chores at home, including chopping firewood and pumping drinking water from the pumps in our backyard.

As a youngster growing up I was intrigued with the surrounding natural beauty of the town, and the old southern oak moss trees were always inspiring. Many of the residents in town planted flowers in their yards, and you could just ride around and see the pretty flowers in bloom in many yards around town. It was primarily a farming community back in the fifties, as many family farms were all over the county. Even with the tremendous growth over the years and the new developments, the town has retained its quaint small town atmosphere and hospitality.

It is still a riverfront town with its' historic old moss trees, churches, schools, cemeteries, historic trails and houses on the National Register of Historic Places. The Conway Marina has a nice long boardwalk right by the banks of the Waccamaw River. You can go for a walk on the boardwalk and pass people fishing, jogging, exercising, as others go cruising by on their boats up and down the Waccamaw River.

There is a Bed and Breakfast near the river with shops and restaurants close by in a revitalized downtown. Whether you are visiting or is a tourist, everything one needs to feel right at home is here in this little quaint riverfront town.

Conway Now – Still a Riverfront Town

This quaint riverfront town is one of the best kept secrets near the Myrtle Beach Grand Strand area. Many people come to visit the Myrtle Beach Grand Strand area each year, as it is a major tourist attraction with much to offer with its many beaches, and many other attractions. But just 14 miles away to the west is that lovely old historic riverfront town of Conway with its many attractions and with much that is different to offer the tourists. One can get a good history of the area and its people, as Conway is the county seat, and the old county courthouse has been beautifully restored.

If you enter Conway over the old Main Street Bridge, it will be a beautiful, scenic, and historic sight as you come across the bridge over the Waccamaw River. You have just crossed the mighty Waccamaw River, one of the few black water rivers in the world, and it comes right by our little quaint town. As you arrive in town over the bridge at the first stop light the building on the left is City Hall, a very historic building. The Visitors Center is just a few doors across from City Hall, and the Visitors Center is where you can get information on tours, etc. You are on your way to enjoying your visit as a tourist and will be able to see history up close with so many historic sites to see, and some are on the National Register of Historic Places.

As you drive down some streets you will have to yield the right of way to large moss laden oak trees in the streets. The oak trees were there first, therefore the paved streets had to just curve around them. There is much to do and see in this historic riverfront town.

The marina is nearby with its boardwalk and riverboat tours, or you can just rent a boat or watercraft. There are many eateries in the area with many types of restaurants, cafes, etc. You can dine outdoors along the river, go sightseeing or go on a guided expedition.

Along with the many eateries, etc. there are some unique shops, a pleasant mix of the old historic downtown revitalization, and various new malls and shopping centers on the outskirts. There are all kinds of shops, including specialty and antique shops along with various other stores and chain restaurants and hotels. Shopping in a small town atmosphere is as memorable as there is delightful dining to go right along with the quaint shops. This riverfront town I call home is still a unique and pleasant mix of "Then and Now" and downtown has been wonderfully revitalized.

The Horry County Museum is on Main Street and contains many historical artifacts, and a wonderful insight into the history of the area, with a display of animals, etc. There are many events and festivals throughout the year that encourage residents to celebrate the culture and history of the area. There are musical events under the Main Street Bridge, and of course there is a big July 4th celebration, and a big Christmas parade, along with various other events and festivals.

There are walking tours that are available where you can see and take in the majestic local history. There is so much to see including historic churches, buildings, restored old homes, cemeteries, etc. There are guided tours along with self guided tours, and the Conway Visitors Center will be able to provide you with all the information you need to enjoy your visit to this quaint lovely old historic riverfront town.

Here you are back in time and history, yet still so close to the Myrtle Beach Grand Strand area and the many beaches, theaters, parks, golf courses, Broadway at the Beach, the Pavilion, Brookgreen Gardens, etc. This riverfront town is here with a different and unique experience for you. The small town atmosphere and hospitality is still here, as it was then and is still now. There is a peace and tranquility where one can enjoy the peace and quiet enjoyment of his home as he sits on the porch on a nice pleasant sunny afternoon. I truly enjoy sitting on my front porch on a peaceful day just reflecting on life, then and now.

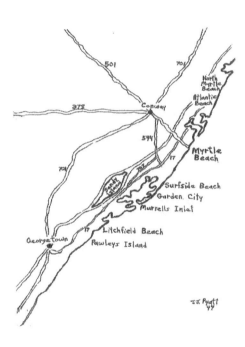

Reflections of Life – Then and Now

A half century ago when I went to school here life was oh so simple then, so to speak. When we finished high school we went away to work or further our education as there were no colleges of technical schools here. Now Conway is the home of Coastal Carolina University, a tremendous university with a great reputation worldwide. Students come to Coastal Carolina University from all over the country and the world, and Coastal Carolina University has great academic and athletic programs. The football and baseball teams were nationally ranked in 2004, and the university has produced some professional players from its athletic programs.

A new football stadium opened last year, and the locals love and are really proud of their university. The university is also expanding to keep up with the increasing demand for entrance by applicants from all over the country and the world. Many students who come to the area to attend the university also relocate here to live and work and pursue careers after they finish their education. They also fall in love with the area and the peoples' hospitality and now call it home.

Conway is also the home of Horry Georgetown Technical College (HGTC) Conway branch, and it is a great technical college and produces some productive and wonderful students. There are plenty of educational opportunities for those who wish to pursue their education and obtain a good job skill and a good career. They are also on-line and some courses are offered online and the courses offered here are as good as any you will find anywhere.

This wonderful and historic old riverfront town has or is within easy reach of everything one could desire to have a wonderful vacation, and enjoy the tourist attractions and get a good history of the area. It truly has a lifestyle of its' own. There is also a wonderful medical center just outside the center of town. When I was growing up in the fifties the hospital was in town on 9th Avenue. My father spent time in the hospital on 9th Avenue and also spent time in the Conway Medical Center.

This riverfront town has a lifestyle of its' own, and ones' days, evenings, and nights can be filled with exciting activities. Over the years as I came back to visit I would often spend my mornings in Conway outdoors seeing the sights of old places, and driving all over this historic riverfront town before going to the Grand Strand beaches in the afternoons. Then I'd return to town and take in a baseball or softball game on a nice summer evening. On other days we would go fishing in the Waccamaw River, and I sure enjoyed those fresh water fish fries that my old baseball teammates would have.

This riverfront town has evolved even more over the years to where it is today, and I have watched it evolved over the four decades since I graduated from high school here. Today it is a tourist delight, and one can now enjoy the benefits of national hotels and restaurant chains in town and on the outskirts of town. Many of them are located on highway 501 between Conway and Myrtle Beach. Highway 501 has always been the major highway between Conway and Myrtle Beach, but now there are many other new highways all over the area. Many of the tourists still come through Conway on highway 501 to get to their vacation destinations at the various beaches.

As a kid I would stand at the corner of highway 501 and Race Path Avenue and watch the cars filled with tourists head to the beaches. Now many of them know about this quaint unique riverfront town and spend part of their vacation here. They now know about this riverfront town and its' many attractions and they detour here and enjoy the benefits of the historic riverfront and marina, and enjoy the many attractions in a peaceful and tranquil setting.

Memories of Early Years

I still enjoy going by the old county courthouse, even though there's a new courthouse in back of it now. The old county courthouse has a lot of history. When I was in high school my homeroom teacher and Civics instructor was Mr. E.A. Finney Jr. and he later became the first black South Carolina Supreme Court Chief Justice since post reconstruction. He took his Civics class to the old courthouse about 1956 to observe a murder trial that was in session. It was an interesting trial with witnesses who saw the crime being committed, and testifying in open court with the circuit judge presiding.

Taking tours of the courthouse was one of the extra curricular activities we engaged in while in school in the mid fifties. We also took a tour of one of the banks downtown in the mid fifties, before electronic banking and ATMs, etc.

There are now monuments on the grounds of the old courthouse honoring veterans of wars and giving honor to its' native sons who have given their life for their country. The courthouse grounds now have many historical markers. The memories of those early years always bring back some special reflections each time I visit some locations.

After migrating away in the early sixties to work and attend college in California, I would always make a point to take the old tours every time I came back to visit. The scenic and historic places always stuck in my mind, and I tried to recapture and retain as many of the old scenes as possible. Over the years and decades much has evolved and changed, but some scenes and historic places only seemed to get better with time.

The river has kept roaring along all these years and is now even a more pleasant place to be near, with much more to do near its banks, with marinas and boardwalks. We locals have always known about our special riverbank locations where the fishes bites best, and where the boating and swimming is best. And for some of us the river provided great and healthy food, especially when it was Shad season. The Shad is an ocean going fish, but at certain times of the year it seeks fresh water to lay its eggs. We knew when that was and had good fishing and Shads in the freezer all year. The river runs wide and long and passes many towns.

The river is not too far from the old courthouse, and the marina is just a few blocks to the rear of the courthouse, as are various shops, restaurants, etc. for your special needs. The downtown area has always been very quaint and unique, and in the heart of the revitalized downtown is where you will see a lot of history.

The old courthouse is only about three blocks from City Hall, and City Hall is just down from the foot of the Main Street Bridge. The Visitor Center is nearby, and across Kingston Street is a lot of history with the Kingston Presbyterian Church, etc. A tremendous amount of history is in these few blocks downtown. Just two blocks down from City Hall on Main Street is the old post office. It was the old post office when I was growing up in the fifties. In front of the old post office is the Wade Hampton oak tree, a site once used for political assemblies. The tree was named after General Wade Hampton.

The old post building later became the home of the Horry County Museum, and the museum will be moving to new quarters down Main Street soon. Across the street from the old post office is the Hut Bible Class, a very historic building on the grounds of the First Methodist Church. A little farther down Main Street is the old Conway High School and the old Burroughs School. I often rode my bicycle past these schools when I was working in the area in the fifties. We lived in the Baggetts Heights neighborhood, and I would ride my bicycle all the way from 9th Avenue and highway 378 down 9th Avenue all the way to Main Street to get to work. The historic old houses that I passed on my bicycle in the fifties are still there today and preserved nicely.

I often took tours when I returned for vacations by driving all the way down Main Street after arriving in town over the Main Street Bridge. I'd go past City Hall, the old post office, the Hut Bible Class, the old Conway High School and all the way out Main Street to highway 701 North. The areas are more developed now because of the tremendous growth over the decades.

14

The golf course is still in the same location on Country Club drive off Main Street beyond the new post office. I often caddied at the golf course to get extra money for school in the fifties. Many of the people and tourists passing through Conway come on highway 501 which is now a major thoroughfare with many shopping centers, hotels, motels, restaurants including national chains, etc. Superstores are now a welcome part of the community and are located inside the city limits. The new Conway High School is also on highway 501 as well as new developments and subdivisions nearby. Tourists won't see these other wonders in this historic riverfront town if they don't venture off highway 501. With a slight detour they will be amazed and pleasantly surprised as to how much this unique riverfront town has to offer tourists and locals alike.

Over the years I have always spent a lot of my vacations in this riverfront town over all the decades since I graduated from high school here. I always appreciated the rivers' unique differences from the ocean and beaches. I grew up loving and having a great deal of respect for the river, and often spent a lot of summers playing by the river when I was very young here. Some days I just go down to the marina and watch the ducks waddle on the river banks or swim in the river, and see the waves in the river as the boats go passing by. It's still a unique and refreshing sight.

Coming into town across the Main Street Bridge

Historic City Hall

Boats at the Marina

The Historic Old County Courthouse

Oak tree on Elm Street

Oak trees on Race Path Avenue

Race Path Avenue

Race Path Avenue has been a special place for me for over half a century. I enjoy playing tourist, especially driving down highway 501 as if going to Myrtle Beach, and as I approach Race Path Avenue I always look to my left and see on the corner of highway 501 and Race Path Avenue the old Cherry Hill Baptist Church. It is awaiting restoration now after all these decades, and the new church is right there beside it. There are many old historic live oak trees there in the churchyard, and the new church was cleverly designed around the magnificent old oak trees. I have been inspired by those old oak trees for over half a century now, and they seem to have a historic story to tell as they alone have seen the many generations come and go.

Race path Avenue has always been a focal point of the Black community, and we still refer to it as the Hill. It was named Race Path because of the horse races that were held there many decades ago. I remember seeing a horse running down Race Path Avenue, followed by a horse and rider chasing the runaway horse over a half century ago. The horse stopped running and was caught not too far from our backyard which was less than two blocks from Race Path Avenue. Things were different back then in what we referred to as the good old days.

The intersection of Race Path Avenue and highway 501 is an intriguing and interesting area even to this day. I can recall the many Sundays over a half century ago that I would stand at the intersection waiting for the light to change so that I could continue on to church a block farther up Race Path Avenue. I could wave at my friends standing on the steps of the old Cherry Hill Church.

The Bethel A.M.E. Church is just a block up from the Cherry Hill Baptist Church, and the Bethel A.M.E. Church is over a century old (rebuilt 1940). Many generations have gone to the same churches, their births, marriages, and death all in the same church. I enjoyed going to that church as I was growing up here, and I still recall those wonderful Jubilee Singers so many decades ago. Many of the elder generations had migrated to Conway from the surrounding country areas to find work and to live in a larger town.

Race Path Ave today still has those majestic old oak trees all the way past the churches to the beginning of the avenue near downtown. On the other end of Race Path Avenue there are also some old oak trees and residential houses. On that end of Race Path Avenue also sits one of the houses that the honorable judge (S.C. Supreme Court Chief Justice) E.A. Finney Jr. once resided in. Every time I pass that house I think of my days in his classroom at the old Whittemore High School. That house is less than three blocks from our back yard, and I often go out our back gate to go up Race Path to what we still call the Hill.

There was a movie theatre on Race Path Avenue back in the fifties that we went to see the western movies. That building has now been renovated and is now a police substation. There was once a hotel and dry cleaning business on Race Path Avenue, different businesses are there today. Our house was only a few blocks away from the Hill section of Race Path Avenue, and it still stands today on the same spot my parents built it on in 1946. Race Path Avenue has been in my life for over a half century, and I still enjoy touring all of the area from one end of the avenue to the other end looking at history.

I also enjoy touring 9th Avenue from one end to the other, especially from 9th Ave. and Race Path Avenue all the way beyond 9th Avenue and Main Street. I took this route to my after school jobs when I was in high school here. I would marvel at the historic old houses on 9th Avenue between highway 501 and Main Street. Today there is a lot more development around these historic old houses, and these historic old houses have been preserved very nicely, some with historic markers in their front yards.

When the weather is nice you can often see the residents working in their yards keeping the flowers and yards looking very nice and groomed. When I passed by these old houses going to work over a half century ago I knew that they would one day be declared historic and were something special. They just seemed to catch my artistic eye, and many of these creations are truly works of art, as any artist would tell you.

I also worked for a time farther down 9th Avenue towards the lake, and that area around the lake was a very beautiful and artistic scene. I would sometimes see an art instructor teaching his students to paint outdoor scenes near the lake. I knew even before then that I too would be an artist, and one day capture the magnificent scenes and history of this unique and one of a kind old historic riverfront town.

Artists and paintings wer4e sort of rare in my neighborhood back then. My teachers in school would get me to use color chalk to draw Christmas scenes on the blackboards during the Christmas season. And in the background of the Christmas scene I would often put a very small scene of a local area, not too obvious.

I subsequently painted watercolor scenes and pastel landscapes of the lake area, and still have a couple that is almost a half century old. They have always hung in my parent's house ever since I painted them while in high school here. I have a ton of experiences and memories here even though I migrated away to work for 42 years. I always retained my deep roots and heritage here, and always came back to visit as often as I could over the decades.

And now that I am retired and here most of the time, it now feels like I never left. I still am more intrigued now with what the area has to offer in greater quantities and quality. There are more tourists and developments with all the things development brings, such as hotels, restaurants, shops, national chains, etc. But some things are still the same, such as the beautiful old moss laden oak trees, the historic churches, cemeteries and peaceful tree lined residential streets, etc. And of course that old man river, that majestic and bold black water river, known as the Waccamaw River. Life near the Waccamaw River has always been wonderful, even to this day.

Life Near the Waccamaw River
Then and Now

The Waccamaw River has a very deep and rich history of its own, and has provided a way of life for an abundance of life in and out of the river. For centuries it has provided for people living near its banks, even from post reconstruction to today. In the early years people and various settlements or communities migrated close to the river to live. The river and inter-coastal waterway was a major route of transportation, and a source of healthy food for the early settlers and inhabitants. The river supported plantations and farms in the early years, and some of the plantations are preserved to this day, and are on other historic tours in the nearby counties.

The Waccamaw River runs pass this historic riverfront town all the way down pass Sandy Island in Georgetown County. The first time I recall seeing the Waccamaw River was when I went to Sandy Island as a small child over a half century ago. I often went from Conway to Sandy Island in the summers when I was young to enjoy the summers while my parents worked. We had to go across the Waccamaw River to get to Sandy Island, and the same is true today as the island is still an isolated island and home to the Gullah people.

My father was born and raised on Sandy Island and migrated to Conway, that lovely old historic riverfront town to work and raise his family. My father would often tell us how he had to go to work at age 13 in 1923 to help raise their family after his father died. As the oldest male child he became the Gullah Chief of Annie Village where they resided on Sandy Island. So that makes me the son of a Gullah Chief.

It was later that he told me that the Waccamaw River runs all the way past Conway to Sandy Island and beyond. Some of the largest riverboats were the ones' most likely to be using the river for long trips transporting goods; or other large fishing boats going to deeper waters for a big catch. We would stand on the banks and watch the boats go by and the same is true today.

We always enjoyed the Waccamaw River on Sandy Island because we could swim and fish close to shore as young children. We didn't have to wade in too deeply since some of us were not very good swimmers at that time. The rivers' inlets were also ideal for planting rice and some small family rice fields were planted at the water's edge. I can remember my grandmother leading the harvest of the rice so many decades ago. We kids were too young to help harvest the rice so we just watched the adults as they harvested the rice. Even after so many decades these wonderful scenes of life on and near the river are still very vivid in my mind. I began to paint some of these scenes of life from so many years ago. An artist sees things differently especially when looking at the natural and pristine riverfront scenes on an isolated island that has remained virtually unchanged for centuries.

There were also the many old moss laden oak trees on the island, the same as you see throughout our old historic riverfront town. Some of the old moss laden oak trees near the river on that isolated island seemed so huge compared to the ones in our riverfront town. Those old moss laden oak trees had nothing or no one to disturb them for years, and no paved streets are there on that isolated island. There is no type of traffic to pollute their beauty.

They can just continue to stand and rest in peace as they have done for centuries, and just watch the generations come and go. Every time I see that old moss laden oak trees on the island I just know that they have seen it all over the centuries, and I would love to hear them tell their stories. The picture of them standing there in majestic grace is one I will never forget, and am thankful that I had the opportunity to see that view of life along the river.

It has been said that a picture speaks a thousand words, so to speak, and I hope my painting of the scenes help some people to pause and think of life so many years ago. Even today, especially in early spring when so many of the flowers are in full color blooming, I visit some streets where it looks like a living watercolor or soft pastel painting by nature itself. All colors are a-blooming in many yards all over town, and especially on some residential streets laden with trees where the residents have kept their yards and shrubbery neatly trimmed. You know it's a good beginning to another spring in the old riverfront town, and everything is getting ready for new life.

Just seeing all the beautiful life like natural color scenes by nature itself is more than enough to get an artist motivated. One can just snap a picture to paint later, or to get out a sketchpad to sketch some of nature's most colorful pictorial scenes to be painted later in the days to come. I always get lots of pictures in my camcorder and sketch book so that I can come back in the days to come and further develop and paint them. That is an added plus to being retired, for one has time in the coming months to record and paint all the incredible, beautiful and historic scenes all over this lovely old historic riverfront town.

28

The early springtime is the time of year when the entire tree lined streets downtown and in the residential areas seem to come more alive and colorful. They are looking their best with the early spring's natural and colorful colors welcoming in a new tourist season that's about to begin. It's always on time every year, and right about the Monday after Easter is when most people begin to look forward to the new season. That is the time of year when the snowbirds (northerners who vacation here during the winter) begin to leave to go back to their homes in the cold weather states. Springtime has always been the time of year when I would pause and deeply reflect about then and now, and chart a course for the future.

Springtime – A Reflection, Then and Now

Easter Monday has traditionally been the day when we began the spring flings, and the beginning of the tourist season in earnest. When I was in high school here we always scheduled our first baseball game for Easter Monday (the Monday after Easter). Easter Monday was the day our official sandlot baseball season began. April and May has always been my favorite time of year to enjoy the new season, and to get outdoors more and enjoy the good colorful months leading into the middle of summer. I have baseball records of games we played here in 1960, and that was a very good year for our Whiz Kids baseball team.

Springtime and early summer has always been my favorite time of year in the Carolina low-country, especially in this historic riverfront town that is still my home base. The springtime was when we began to wake up, so to speak, from our quasi hibernation from the winter months. It was a time for us to get out and get in shape by doing natural exercises on the athletic field. We didn't have cable TV in the fifties and didn't have all the distractions and bombardment with certain TV programs and ads, etc. enough said. We weren't the type to buy all kinds of equipment on TV today that we didn't need in order to get in shape and stay in shape.

There are some youngsters today who are in worst shape than we in. It didn't take us long to get in shape either, as most of us did not drink or smoke in those days, and we were not afraid of a hard day's work. Some days were hot but we were in such excellent condition that we would just keep on running and playing ball, even in the heat of the day.

We were in much better shape than the sit down TV youngsters of today, where many of them are constantly out of shape. I often came back over the years to visit, and in the 1980s' we would have old timers' games where we so-called old guys would play the teenagers. One day we had a softball game scheduled for 7:00PM and there was a slight heat wave that week. We old timers took infield practice and I noticed that the young teenagers were standing under the trees in the shade. We old timers were in shape and had prepared for the heat. When it came time for the teenagers to take their infield practice they just remained under the trees in the shade.

We played the game and we old timers beat the teenagers so bad that their little girlfriends sitting in the stands started to get on us old timers. We beat them so bad that their little girlfriends had to come onto the field after the game to comfort them. They were so upset that we beat their boyfriends so bad that they challenged us to a rematch with them on the condition that we old timers bat the opposite of our natural sides. We agreed to their challenge and we played a few days later and beat them almost as bad as we had beaten their boyfriends. They were so upset that one of them took my baseball cap and just crushed and pushed it permanently out of shape.

As I came back over the years it was always just like old times, and lots of fun. In fact I took most of my vacations here and didn't have a great desire to go anywhere else. I got to go to various other cities on business or for classes as my job sent me to various cities over the years. It was wonderful to have a job that afforded me the opportunity to visit other cities across the country.

I was having the best of both worlds, and I chose to return to my roots after I retired in order to continue on in the tradition of good, clean, healthy living near the Waccamaw River in this lovely old historic riverfront town.

As I pause and reflect on life, then and now, it's sometimes gets to be a thin line unless I pause a little more. Some of the things I did decades ago I still do now, although now most of my getting around town is in my car and not on my bicycle. And when I go to certain stores I have to look up at the signs and remind myself that it's the same location of the other store that used to be here years ago. The downtown area is still fairly small, but wonderfully revitalized, and continues to bring back memories of so many decades ago as I rode my bicycle all over the downtown area and beyond.

Many of the buildings, houses, etc. are still there, but different people are there now, and sometimes it's the next generation coming on. I ride through many of the neighborhoods to see if some of the same people are still there. We still have class reunions, etc. but not everyone is able to make it after all these years, and you may only see them in their neighborhood enjoying life just as they have been doing for decades. I cruise through many neighborhoods to take in the beautiful scenery and sometimes don't notice the people there.

Springtime is the time of year for many outdoor activities, including golf, tennis, boating, and sports. There is a very large and nice tennis complex at the marina and its many tennis courts can accommodate many. There is also a large and modern softball complex a little off highway 501 in an area that used to be a farm; it's a peaceful and tranquil setting in springtime.

Moss Laden Oak Trees Abound All Over

A Peaceful and Tranquil Scene

Historic Churches

Oak Trees in My Neighborhood

Old Tobacco Barns are Fading Away Fast

Springtime – Peace and Tranquility

Springtime is no longer the time to gear up for the farm season. Many of the farms are no longer in existence now after so many changes over the decades. But there are still some old tobacco barns standing around on the outskirts of town here and there. I see these old barns telling a deep part of history and life as it was in the county decades ago. Many of us worked on farms at some point in our lives as we were growing up here, as it was quite common to work on farms during the summer when you got old enough.

There is also a different type of peace and tranquility in the springtime, as it is a little quieter with school still in session, less tourists traveling through the area going to the various beaches on the Myrtle Beach Grand Strand. It is totally opposite from the early fall when there is a decrease in the number of tourists and school is back in session. It is sort of a quiet time in the county, and time to prepare for the cooler weather a-coming.

The two seasons compliment each other naturally as the fall season turns to winter, and the greenery turns to brown as the leaves begin to fall from the trees. It's like nature is telling its natural environment to relax, slow down and rest until early springtime. Then we repeat the process again with all the wonderful tourists who will surely come back again. Each year they come to enjoy our lovely old riverfront town and its natural and surrounding beauty. They know that they will not be able to see or enjoy what they see and get in this riverfront town no where else on earth. There is a special type of peace and tranquility that you can only get near the river.

There is no better place to be than by the Waccamaw River in our tranquil and hospitable riverfront town with all it has to offer. There has always been something special about riverfront towns and communities up and down the river. It seems as if they march not to a different drum or drummer, but to a special and peaceful and tranquil flowing of the mighty river. Even when the river is roaring with the wind and waves there's an inward inner calm that one that is living near the river comes to recognize.

The people in time seem to acquire some of this contentment and inner peace which manifests itself in a special and unique type of down home hospitality. A different type of hospitality has always been known to exist in certain small southern towns. It is a type of neighborly atmosphere that you do not find in the cities or larger towns. These people are truly different and real in their beliefs and genuine in their hospitality. It is something one has to experience for themselves in order to fully comprehend it and appreciate it.

The Peoples' Hospitality

Even as I was growing up here many decades ago I recognized that there was a natural and unique hospitality in the area, especially among the people who lived and interacted so closely with the river. I spent a lot of my early summers visiting and living with relatives on the sea island, where we spent many days by the river banks. The river provided food, entertainment, and healthy outdoor activities for naturally keeping in shape.

I deeply believe that such hospitality is deeply rooted in the area being a historically Bible Belt Community. There still is, and has always been something unique and intangible about such Bible Belt Communities. Even though we now live in a 21st century technological society, the effects of the Bible Belt traditions are still obvious, and can be felt and seen in the demeanor and hospitality of the people. People in the communities are still friendly and treat each other as neighbors.

As I cruise through the various communities and neighborhoods, the people, both young and old, will wave and speak as I pass. I sometimes sit on my front porch enjoying life on a nice day, and the people passing by walking to and fro will always speak, even though I don't know the majority of them. I only returned to live here after I retired after being away for over four decades, but the peoples' hospitality makes it seem like I never really left. I was so accustomed to city life where people seldom speak to you as you pass them by. I had to pinch myself to remind myself that it is O'K to speak, and to be more hospitable in this community and environment.

It is truly different from the city life and city atmosphere that I spent over four decades working in and living in. I always experienced the hospitality when I visited here over the years and decades that I was away living in the city. But somehow I assumed it might just be isolated instances of hospitality. But now I am convinced by being here full time and witnessing it for myself over a sustained period of time.

I would come to visit over the years and when I went to gas up my car I would go inside the gas station to pay before gassing up. I was surprised when the gas station attendants told me to go pump the gas and fill up and then come back inside and pay for the gas. This is something I had never experienced in all my years in the city. In the city it was mandatory that you paid for the gas before you pumped the gas into your car. It took me a while to get comfortable putting gas into my car before paying for it. In some places it is still that way today.

I always experienced the hospitality even when I visited here over the years and decades that I was away working in the city. But somehow I assumed it might just be isolated instances of hospitality, but now I am convinced by the constant experiences and by being here full time, and witnessing it for myself over a sustained period of time.

It has often been said that if you're nice to people that some of it will eventually rub off even on people who are not so nice. That's the way true hospitality works also, because even though I was away all those years the more I experienced the hospitality of the people, the more I made a concerted effort to practice good hospitality, and feel right at home as if I had never left even after all these years.

In the old days growing up here in the 1950's it was more natural to be hospitable because that's how we were raised here in our communities. There were many smaller communities in those days; therefore it was a lot easier as everyone knew most everyone. Sometimes we would have a difficult time getting enough guys together to play a sandlot baseball game.

Neighborhoods now are about the same size but with a lot more people living in the various communities. In the old days you could pass by a lot of woods going to certain neighborhoods even in town. When going from my neighborhood to the golf course to work we would walk long distances and sees nothing but woods. Today there has been tremendous development all along the highways and byways and back-roads that we once referred to as country back woods. There are housing developments all over in what used to be heavily wooded areas.

But throughout all the development and increased number of people, there is still the deeply rooted and ingrained hospitality so unique to this area. Some of the people of the neighborhoods were living there when I was growing up here. Some others are people I went to school with who never left here, and have called this lovely old riverfront town their home all their life. It has been stated that a certain percent of people will not leave home after they finish high school, and I'm sure that percentage is even higher in towns close to the river, such as our lovely old historic riverfront town.

A New Generation of Kids Play Outdoors

Looking Up Main Street, with the Main Street
Bridge in the Background

Crossing Over the Main Street Bridge

Old Oak Tree Across from City Hall

Another Look up Historic Main Street

Historic Houses and Places

Courthouse Monument and the Vietnam
Memorial on the Courthouse Grounds

The Historic Bethel A.M.E. Church

The River at the Conway Marina

The Pull of the River Keeps Calling

The Pull of the River

There is something about the pull of the river, especially if you grew up near the river, and spent your early childhood living and playing near the banks of a roaring river such as the mighty Waccamaw River. No matter where you go to work or live there's a part of you that can feel the river pulling you back home. There's a part in everyone that yearns to relive some of the good old days of yesteryear. Especially after spending so many years in the city with all its concrete, and the enclosed atmosphere one has to live in

The environment near the river has always been wonderful; a place where one can enjoy the wide-open peaceful banks of the river. We used to go swimming in the river under the Main Street Bridge years ago, as we just slipped in and no one would see us there. It was therapeutic then, and it is even more therapeutic now that there is a lot more stress on people in our current day society. Nature has always been the best source of stress release as it is wholly natural.

That is perhaps one of the major reasons so many tourists come to the Myrtle Beach Grand Strand area on their vacations. This area is where they can have fun, relax and relieve their stresses from the world of work and what not. I have spent many afternoons by the river and the Atlantic Ocean with its beautiful beaches in splendid peace and tranquility. Being that close to nature in a serene environment is totally relaxing with a complete release of stresses. There is so much to do near the water, with many attractions to help the tourists enjoy themselves, as they are relaxing in or near our wonderful lovely old historic riverfront town.

Many tourists come and go each season, and seasons come and go. But the river just keeps rolling along day after day with its tremendous pull calling here true lovers home. There is always concern that with the tremendous growth in the areas that it will somehow, somewhere, affect the quality of life in and near the river. The river has provided a quality of life for an abundance of life that has depended on the river for its existence for centuries.

Development is continuing on an unprecedented scale unlike any that has come before to this quaint riverfront town. Development can be good for communities and mean great progress when planned for and managed efficiently. There can be a balance between growth and environment, as there will always be something that some people would like to preserve as dear to their heart. I would hate to see development out of control and destroy the beauty of our little quaint unique riverfront town. It is not like it was when I was growing up here many decades ago, as many things have changed for the better. This is a testament to the good and hospitable forward thinking people of the town and surrounding areas.

Much great progress has occurred and there are more good things and events to come to this wonderful riverfront town. But there are some challenges ahead, and I'm sure that the good and hospitable forward thinking people of our wonderful riverfront town are prepared to meet such challenges, and continue to make this area a wonderful place for everyone. Challenges are a part of progress and all forward thinking people are prepared for challenges on the path to progress.

The Challenges Ahead

After many decades of working and living in the city in California I decided to return to my roots here in this little town by the river. My visits over the years had convinced me that this is the place where I would be able to enjoy the peace and quiet enjoyment of the community and surrounding areas. I would also be close to that wonderful Waccamaw River and the nice beaches all up and down the Myrtle Beach Grand Strand area. It was near the river that I had such wonderful memories so many years ago. I knew that a smaller peaceful town would not have some of the problems of the city, or at least not on the same large scale.

Over the years I became convinced that the problems of the city were due in part because some youngsters were not raised in the environment that I was raised in. Our ancestors succeeded with a lot less, so I really didn't have an excuse that I could use to not succeed. Dropping out of school never entered my mind, but it is a major problem with many youngsters all over the country, especially in the inner city, where I was living. I could not tolerate dropping out and hanging out and being uneducated, because I believe in progress. It is refreshing to see so much progress that this riverfront town has made over the decades.

When I went to school here in the 1950's our little school didn't have the best or latest equipment and materials; but we were committed and became educated and functionally literate. I did not have any problems getting into and graduating from the California State University System, and having a successful and rewarding career.

And now I've made it to this wonderful point in time to enjoy my retirement here in this riverfront town where it all began decades ago. It is a lame excuse to continue to blame ones' failure on bad schools, although some schools are better than others. We can do as our ancestors did, succeed in spite of obstacles in your path. We had after school study sessions to reinforce or go over materials that there wasn't enough time to cover in class. Study sessions made some things clearer after classes and serve a purpose even today. There are various tutorial programs in the community for students who truly want to apply themselves and learn. There is also a tremendous amount of information on-line on the internet on many web sites.

Things have changed over the years, and we now live in a 21st century technological society. The youth of today have more educational opportunities, more economic opportunities, and unlimited access to information online. My generation had limited opportunities, but we succeeded and a growing number of us are returning to retire here by the Waccamaw River in various communities. This will give us more time to help some youths of today who seem to believe that dropping out and hanging out is a panacea. They must be prepared to compete in the Global Economy, and there is no acceptable excuse for not acquiring a job skill, and becoming a productive and responsible citizen just like their ancestors. Our ancestors succeeded with a lot less, and so can you. They were very resourceful and had a vision and goals, and were dedicated and worked hard to achieve their goals.

A Vision with Goals and Objectives

You must keep focused on and keep pursuing your Goals and Objectives, and keep your Goals and Objectives in your vision. With the many distractions of today bombarding the young generation it seems to be very easy to become Stuck in the Mud-pile with drop out logic. This type of nonsense will keep you permanently on the bottom of the economic ladder, and you will never be able to retire and enjoy the many good things this area has to offer.

This area is growing fast here by the Waccamaw River, with many conveniences and nice houses for people seeking the good life. This area has everything one needs, but you must stay in school and become prepared to compete in the Global and National Economies. People from all over the country and world are migrating here to this area because of the wonderful quality of life this area offers. They will be prepared to enjoy the good life here, and so must you.

The vision you see must be real and predicated on a real-time view of this 21st century technological society we now live in. Everyone must study and work to get ahead, and that is a sure-fire way to get ahead today. If you drop out and hang out with a bunch of people going nowhere fast; you will end up going the same place they're going. It doesn't matter what your beliefs are, faith without works is dead (James 2:17-26, II Timothy 2:15). With the opportunities in this 21st century technological society, no able bodied person should remain in poverty; the destruction of the poor is their poverty (Proverbs 10:15). Success comes to those who actively seek it, and are not afraid of work.

Study and work so that you can obtain your fair share of benefits, and own your own land and avoid remaining in poverty. "The man that tilleth his land shall have plenty of bread, but he that followeth after vain persons shall have poverty enough" (Proverbs 28:19). Study and work and be successful in this new Global Economy! You can be the head and not the tail, above and not beneath; IF, you fulfill the Condition Precedent in Deuteronomy 28:13! This is a guarantee!

Doing the right thing always works, and even nature itself teaches us right from wrong. Dropping out and hanging out will not improve your educational position or increase your economic opportunities or potentials. We can use the churches if need be to tutor at night and on weekends, as the struggle continues. Our ancestors succeeded with a lot less, and so can you with all of today's opportunities.

Missed educational opportunities while you are young will be felt in a detrimental manner your entire lifetime. There is value in Study and Work, and you will learn a lot about life and yourself. You must overcome obstacles and do for self, as no one is coming to help or save foolish people. I wish I had the educational and economic opportunities that the youth of today have when I was growing up here. It is possible for some students to be very smart, and you may be able to help teach yourself if some classes fall behind in their presentations. I read all of my textbooks from front to back when I went to school here in the 1950's, and I learned some things the teachers didn't get time to teach in class. I learned quite a bit at the old Whittemore schools. Study and Work as there is great value in work, and have Goals and a Vision.

HAVE GOALS AND A VISION
Remain Focused on Goals and Objectives

A man must come out of darkness and find his way into the light; but if he relies on himself to find his way out he may linger forever in his darkness. We need not fear for we too have the covenant (Genesis 9:11 and Deuteronomy 9:11). And Christ is our High Priest (Hebrews 9:11).

We must remain focused on our Goals and Objectives, and keep your Goal in your Vision! From Concept to Completion!

Visualize from layout to development to successful completion, and keep working toward your Goals and Objectives!

Setbacks may come, and obstacles may be placed in your way, but, keep working toward your Goals and Objectives!

It may take a while to set and lay a complete and solid foundation, but don't despair, keep working toward your Goals and Objectives!

Maintain – Credibility and a Commitment to proceed and achieve, and you will succeed and achieve and produce a Quality Product.

You must have Credibility and a Commitment to proceed until you accomplish your Goals and Objectives.

If you maintain Credibility and Commitment, all else will come naturally.

Remember, we were instructed millenniums ago to Study and Work!

T.J. Pyatt

OUR ANCESTORS SUCCEEDED WITH A LOT LESS
You Too Can Succeed With What You Have

Our ancestors succeeded with what little they had and became successful, productive, and responsible and law abiding citizens. They achieved in spite of having limited educational and economic opportunities, and limited access to information. That did not deter them from seeking a better life, and studying and working to be productive and successful. They often went to one room schools, but they retained their quest for knowledge, and became literate and functional.

Many of our youth of today are functionally illiterate, even though we live in a 21st century technological society, with much more than our ancestors had.

The youth of today have much more:
1. Unlimited Educational Opportunities
2. Unlimited Economic Opportunities, and more
3. Access to information (Internet)

Yet a large number of them (over 50% in some areas) drop out of high school as if it's not for them. They end up functionally illiterate because of opportunities squandered, and then they complain about everything including the relevancy of the education or educational system. There are serious problems with certain educational systems in certain areas, but dropping out of school with just hanging out being the only alternative is not the solution. Some schools appear to be nothing more than drop out factories or prep schools for the prison system, but to just drop out and hang out is not an acceptable alternative.

My generation went to separate schools over 50 years ago and we didn't have all the latest or best materials, but we knew we had to become literate and functional. After we became literate and functional in our little schools many of us went on to the best universities throughout the country. One must have the discipline in order to achieve in situations or environments that are not optimum. My generation didn't have the discipline problem that exists with so many of today's youth. In my school days any adult in the community could discipline a child if the parent was not around. Some of the parents today are apparently too uncivilized to discipline the children; and some of them will do you harm if you try to discipline their kids, as some of these parents are hooked on drugs, alcohol and untold follies.

There is a major discipline problem with some of the youngsters among us in our communities. Sending undisciplined youngsters to schools of their choice or their parent's choice will not solve the problem, or enable them to learn and become functionally literate. Even parents with disciplined youngsters who send their children to schools of choice will still have the danger of their children interacting and playing with these undisciplined youngsters in our neighborhoods. And it's just a short matter of time before the good kids are corrupted by the few undisciplined kids in our neighborhoods. Therefore, everyone in the community, even parents with good kids has a stake in the outcome; riding the community of these undisciplined youngsters.

These undisciplined youngsters have a detrimental effect on their good peers and a negative impact on all youngsters in the neighborhood. They are constantly trying to get their peers to drop out of school and just hang out and around with them, engaging in lazy nonsense. These undisciplined youngsters are continuing to turn our neighborhood schools into drop out factories and prep schools for the prison system. They have created and adding to a sub-culture that cherishes being ignorant and uneducated.

The men in these affected communities must stand up, step up, speak up and stand tall. If these undisciplined youngsters continue to refuse to listen, then we should make sure that they become adequately acquainted with our jails, detention centers and prison system.

My generation supposedly went to so called sub par schools but we had a burning desire to learn and get ahead, and we were literate and functional when we graduated. So it's a lazy excuse to say that you cannot learn in your environment in your neighborhood. All schools will never be equal and some injustices may linger forever, but you can and should still achieve in spite of such obstacles. Wealthy neighborhoods have always had better equipped schools, and all parents have a right to give their children every legal competitive edge as possible. (The Constitution does not prohibit wealth discrimination) to put it bluntly.

I can study in my neighborhood just as the wealthy person can study in their neighborhood. My small computer will get me access to the World Wide Web for information just as an expensive computer in a mansion. Most of my writings and books are done on a small inexpensive computer, but that does not prohibit or stop me from producing a quality product. It doesn't matter whether your house is a mansion on a hill or a cottage in the flatlands, you must still study in order to achieve. A debit or a credit is the same no matter where you learn it. The same Income Statement or Balance Sheet will read the same no matter where you read them, in a mansion or in a hut.

You can learn no matter where you are. If my generation had waited until all injustices ceased before we studied we would be waiting until our dyeing day. You can succeed in spite of any lingering injustices, and set the example by excellence. Many of my generation that went to segregated schools are now successfully retired living the good life. There may be no perfect schools in our neighborhoods, but you can and should succeed.

The Struggle Continues –
In our heyday, the church was the focal point in our struggle for civil rights. The church is still the only institution in our community; and will be and must be the focal point in implementing change that will solve the discipline problem with too many of the undisciplined youngsters in our communities. Other ethnic communities own their own restaurants and other businesses in their communities which enable their communities to obtain economic autonomy.

In our community we only have the church as our only institution, and some churches may have also strayed somewhat over the years. But the church is the only institution in our community that we can use as a focal point for change. The churches opened their doors to us many nights and weekends during our civil rights struggle. And those same doors may need to be opened again at night and weekends so our youngsters can get a

64

better understanding of their culture and heritage, and struggles their ancestors had to endure so that they can have a better day. We can teach our youngsters to be literate and functional even if some of the schools cannot.

Sending undisciplined youngsters to schools of choice will not give them what they need to know to improve their self esteem, and be productive and responsible. The road to success will always be lumpy and bumpy as long as they keep digging holes in the road to progress in our communities. Undisciplined conduct is also a drag on the economic revitalization of our communities. Some injustices may linger, but we must continue on to success.

Our Ancestors Succeeded With a Lot Less! You Too Can Succeed!

T.J. Pyatt

65

**Our Ancestors Succeeded with a Lot Less
You too can succeed with what you have**

There is a very deep and rich history for us all to
be proud of as our ancestors paved the way for
us to have a better day with what we have today.

The Rose Hill Memorial Gardens,
A Historic Cemetery

An Old Cemetery on Taylor Square,
Overgrown but not forgotten

The Old Moss Laden Oak Trees Have Been a
Favorite of Generations for Years

Many Generations Have Called the County
Home for Centuries, and have worked Hard to
make it Better for those who follow.

May Such Resolve Continue on to Future
Generations.

The Historic Old Cherry Hill Baptist Church
Was the Church Home for many Generations

The Wade Hampton Oak Tree in front of the
Old Post Office

The Historic Old Burroughs School

New Schools now abound where Old Schools
existed with so many memories years ago

Memories, Memories of Decades Ago
In this Riverfront Town

New Generations Have Come and Others will
follow in their footsteps by the River

You Can Make it Better for All

In spite of any obstacles in the road you must travel in your sojourn here, you too can make it better for all that will follow. We have much more to do and a long way to go, and "there is no free ride"; and if each one does a little, together we can accomplish a lot.

It has been said that one's man's view of the world and life is often described as seen from the perspective he finds himself in, or has succumbed to. It is easy to see things only from one's own vantage point, but one must pause and listen to that choir deep within his conscience. We can all be committed to progress and achievement in the tradition of the elder generations who accomplished so much with so little.

We can do what needs to be done in our neighborhoods in this Riverfront Town to make our communities even better. We can study and work and acquire the necessary job skills to be productive and responsible in the national and global economies.

I remember my early years in the county going to school and studying and working hard, and we made the most of what little we had at that time. It prepared the way for a better day and a better life. My experiences at the Whittemore schools prepared me well for the challenges that I was to face in the decades to come. The Whittemore experience was unique and exciting and will always be a part of me; with its many memories of so many decades ago.

The Whittemore High School Experience

I will be forever grateful that I had the opportunity to have the Whittemore schools mold my character at a young age. The Whittemore experience was unique and spiritually rewarding, and I truly enjoyed life in the Whittemore community.

Whittemore High School was more than a school, it was a self stained community and a way of life. It was a major focal point along with the churches in the Race Path and surrounding communities. Parents who didn't have the opportunity to get a high school education during their youth, sacrificed so that their children could get a good education at Whittemore High School. This was life in the 1950's when I attended the Whittemore schools.

Whittemore High School produced some outstanding citizens of America and the world. Whittemore alumni's are doctors, lawyers, nurses, college professors, health care workers, chemists, scientists, artists, athletes, accountants, business and community leaders, and many more. Mr. Rhue was the principal when I first started at the Whittemore schools, Mr. Lewis became principal in the early 1950's. Mr. E.A. Finney Sr. was the principal from about the mid 1950's to the mid 1960's, then Mr. R.L. Laney became principal until Whittemore was consolidated into Conway High School in 1970.

Whittemore built character and had some dedicated teachers who were genuinely interested in the students getting a good education. They prepared us well for the challenges of the world. People cared about and helped each other out in those days.

When parents were at work they could feel assured that other parents in the community would check on their kids. Whittemore was the main focal point in the community when I was growing up there. Students came from many parts of town to go to Whittemore, places such as, Grainger Town, Tinker Town, Sugar Hill, Tin Top Alley, Spivey Alley, and the Hill or Race Path. Students also came from surrounding towns, such as, Aynor, Gallivants Ferry, Burgess, Bucksport, Homewood, Pine Island, Myrtle Beach, Sand ridge, and many local routes.

Athletics was also a big part of Whittemore High School. There were the football, basketball, and baseball teams. Those Whittemore Bulldogs, I can still see them now, in their purple and gold uniforms. During the football season we'd have a homecoming parade before the homecoming football game. The parade started at Whittemore and went up highway 378 to Racepath Avenue, unto Fifth Avenue, unto Main Street through downtown, passing the old county courthouse, and back down highway 378 to Whittemore. The Homecoming Queen and Miss Whittemore rode in the parade, and the band played and marched all the way.

Homecoming was a time to see and get together with the many former students who had migrated away to work and live. Many of our homecoming games would be against our top rival, Howard High School from Georgetown. Howard High had some very good and tough athletes, and many of them went on to play professional football. At football games, we just stood on the sidelines to watch the games, because we had no grandstands to sit on. Games were played on Friday afternoons, as the field didn't get lights until 1957.

I can also remember the high school basketball games being played on dirt courts. It would sometimes get cold and windy, but we would just bundle up and keep on watching our Bulldogs. The gymnasium wasn't built until about 1954. There was a high school baseball team in the early 1950's. In the late 1950's the baseball team around town was Billy McCloud's Conway Redlegs. I remember them playing a semi pro team called the Raleigh Tigers in 1959, and they split a two game series.

We played a lot of sandlot baseball games on the old Whittemore athletic field, and had many great games there. The summers were hot, but we usually played all summer, until very late in the afternoon. We got together a team of us young teenagers in 1960 and called ourselves the Conway Whiz Kids. Those Whiz Kids were a pretty good team, our first game was against the Conway Redlegs and we lost. But we played the Redlegs two more times that year, and won the city championship by beating the Redlegs.

We played teams from all over the area, from Lake City to Georgetown to Dillion and many others. The Whiz Kids were beating all teams from near and far, and was the talk of the town. People came from near and far to see the Whiz Kids play. It was fun growing up in the Whittemore community in those days. We didn't have a lot but we had each other. Sometimes we'd leave campus and go to Wright's grocery to buy lunch or a snack. Wright's grocery was conveniently located on the corner of Brown Street and Highway 378 (Wright Blvd.).

I have made a personal special tribute to Whittemore by creating a web site to the memory of Dear old Whittemore; at www.whittemorehigh.com

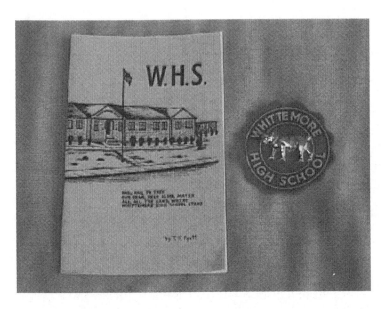

Memories of so many years ago

The Old Whittemore High School
My Dear, Dear Old Alma Mater

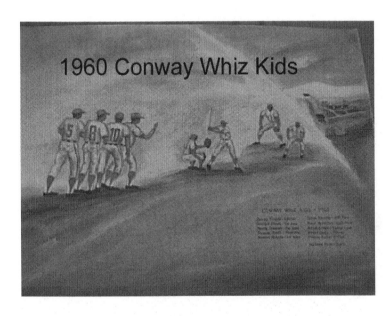

The 1960 Conway Whiz Kids
A truly great semi-pro team of their time

After my season with the Conway Whiz Kids I
ended up in San Francisco at my drawing board
on New Montgomery Street

A Long Journey and Reflections
Of Life, Then and Now

I have lived and worked in large so called progressive cities. But I have never lived in a community with as much unity as the Whittemore community.

My experiences at the old Whittemore schools prepared me well to compete in the world I had to face and exist in. The "Secrets for Success" are not hidden, and you will find them with study and work.

SECRETS FOR SUCCESS

Acquire Economic Skills! Pray & Work
Go to School! – Stay in School!
Do For Self! – Forget About Shortcuts.
Acquire Expertise and Experience. Work Experience!

PRODUCTION:
Acquire Economic Skills!
Produce Quality Products & Services
Obtain Ownership & Control of
Economic Entities (Yours)

DISTRIBUTION:
Marketing – Advertising

CONSUMERS:
Retail
Turn Over $ Dollars in Your Community

Remain Focused on Goals and Objectives.
Use a Systematic and Step-by-Step Approach to
complete huge tasks.
Constantly Probe and Analyze – Utilize a Real Time
Action Plan.
Clearly Define the Problem and Carefully
Analyze the Facts.

Don't be systematically manipulated into economic
dependency on others outside the community.
Acquire Economic Autonomy!

BE PREPARED TO COMPETE
IN THE GLOBAL ECONOMIC ARENA
(And Stay Prepared)

The Global Economic Arena is now before us and The Economic Playing Field has been dictated to us. We must be prepared to Compete in it!

- Identify Potential Job Opportunities (categories) in the Global Economy.
- Identify Economic Skills needed in the Global Economy.
- Acquire Economic Skills (not just degrees) needed in the Global Economy. (Identify your strengths and weaknesses – Reason for leaving last job?)
- Establish Priorities and engage in Economic Networking. (Have Long Term Economic Goals). Avoid that which is Contrary to Sound Doctrine.
- Obtain and Maintain the Proper **A.C.E.** (Attitude -Conduct – Environment).

> **A**ttitude - Must be conducive to Accomplishments.
> **C**onduct - Don't Engage in Conduct Detrimental to Progress.
> **E**nvironment – Avoid Negative Influences and Bad Associations.

Being computer literate is essential for learning and may help you stay ahead of the curve. You can do research online and keep up with the latest technology and financial markets. Information is online. Maintain an up to date resume. You may even have to e-mail your resume.

In every economy in the world there is a need for good financial record keepers, accounting and bookkeeping. Other skills are also needed and in demand, such as, paralegals, medical assistants, auto mechanics, electricians, plumbers, sales, etc. The economy may be down now with high unemployment, and companies are not hiring. There are many skilled and management people looking for work. Some are even going back to college and making it harder for some first time students to get accepted into college. Colleges and Universities all over the land are receiving more applications than they can accept. Many are becoming discouraged and dropping out of the job market. Different Economic Skills are now needed in the Global Economy.

Don't give up, know who you are, stay committed and prepared. Continue to send out resumes and continue to update and upgrade your Economic Skills. You may take classes at night or online. So be prepared as you may end up starting your own company or business. Continue to turn over dollars in your community as this will help create jobs. Be prepared for your opportunity because in the darkest arena a flickering of light will shine showing you your opportunity. Be Prepared!

As new generations are now emerging
to face the challenges that prior generations
faced and conquered because they were
prepared well to face the world.
May they march on to success!

Looking up Race Path Avenue

As I go strolling all over this Old Historic Riverfront Town some things look pretty much the same as they did decades ago. You can still fell the fresh air on a nice day as you go strolling down the streets of old moss laden oak trees or walking along the banks of the Waccamaw River.

The Waccamaw River still runs and roars as it
has for prior generations

The mighty Waccamaw River is a major black water river, and has provided pleasure and food for generations that grew up in and around this Old Historic Riverfront Town.

I journeyed away but kept feeling the pull of the river calling me home.

The Old Oak Tree Watches Over City Hall

The Conway Marina by the Waccamaw River

That View – Then and Now

That is the View, or Recollections of Life, Then and Now, as seen from my perspective or vantage point, in looking at and experiencing life in that lovely Old Historic Riverfront Town.

Our unique experiences and commitment to achievement can make the world a better place because of our efforts to make life and living better for all we have had the opportunity to come in contact with.

Our life's work should be a living legacy to all those who knew us as we journeyed on our sojourn here among them.

Art Director –
T.J. Pyatt
www.tjpyatt.com

98

Index

Made in the USA
Middletown, DE
20 November 2024

65053623R00060